hanuman

Anjana and Kesari, the chief of monkeys, were happily married but they didn't have a child. They decided to pray to Lord Shiva for a son. Lord Shiva was impressed by their devotion and asked Lord Vayu, the wind god, to bless the couple with a child.

Soon, Anjana gave birth to a beautiful baby boy, Hanuman. His parents were very happy. Hanuman was a very naughty boy, and would play many pranks on his mother. But he loved his mother dearly.

One day, Hanuman was playing in his room alone. He went to the balcony and looked up. He saw the sun and thought that it was a big ripe mango!

He loved to eat mangoes, so he decided to eat the mango that he saw in the sky. He extended his hands, and without his knowledge he started to fly!

When Lord Vayu saw this, he rushed in and carried Hanuman in his arms into a cave.

Lord Indra struck Hanuman with lightening. Hanuman was injured and fell down on earth, unconscious.

When Lord Indra, the god of thunder and lightening, saw Hanuman flying towards the sun, he became very angry.

He flew up, up and up
towards the sun, thinking that
it was a huge, ripe mango.

The living beings on earth started suffering as there was no air left. Lord Vayu refused to return to earth and provide air, as he was very unhappy.

All the gods then approached Lord Brahma for help. He then asked Lord Indra to seek forgiveness from Lord Vayu.

Lord Brahma, along with Lord Indra and other gods, went to the cave and humbly asked for forgiveness. To appease him further, they revived Hanuman and showered him with many blessings and powers.

Hanuman was very happy. He returned home to his anxious mother and hugged her. Lord Vayu, too, returned to earth and provided air for the living beings.

The naughty Hanuman spots the sun while playing.

He thinks it is a ripe mango. He loves mangoes so he tries to grab it.

He then starts to fly!

Guess what happens next?

Reprinted in 2016 by

OM KIDZ

An imprint of Om Books International

Corporate & Editorial Office
A-12, Sector 64, Noida 201 301, Uttar Pradesh, India, Phone: +91 120 477 4100
Email: editorial@ombooks.com, Website: www.ombooksinternational.com

Sales Office
107, Ansari Road, Darya Ganj, New Delhi 110 002, India, Phone: +91 11 4000 9000
Fax: +91 11 2327 8091, Email: sales@ombooks.com, Website: www.ombooks.com

Retold by Shreya Mukherjee | Illustrated by Salil Anand, Manoj, Naveen

ISBN: 978-93-82607-22-9

Printed in India

10 9 8 7 6 5 4 3

OM KIDZ

An imprint of Om Books International

ISBN 978-93-82607-22-9

9 789382 607229

www.ombooksinternational.com